MAKING WORD GIFTS

Previous collections by Richard Kell

Fantasy Poets 35 (pamphlet, Oxford 1957)
Control Tower (1962)
Differences (1969)
Humours (1978)
Heartwood (pamphlet, 1978)
The Broken Circle (1981)
In Praise of Warmth, New & Selected (1987)
Rock and Water (1993)
Collected Poems (2001)
Under the Rainbow (2003)
Letters to Enid (2004)
Taking a Break (2008)
Hilarity and Wonder (2011)
Old Man Answering (2014)

MAKING WORD GIFTS

RICHARD KELL

All rights reserved. No part of this work covered by the copyright herein may be reproduced or used in any means – graphic, electronic, or mechanical, including copying, recording, taping, or information storage and retrieval systems – without written permission of the publisher.

Printed by imprintdigital
Upton Pyne, Exeter
www.digital.imprint.co.uk

Typesetting, cover photograph and cover design by narrator
www.narrator.me.uk
info@narrator.me.uk
033 022 300 39

Published by Shoestring Press
19 Devonshire Avenue, Beeston, Nottingham, NG9 1BS
(0115) 925 1827
www.shoestringpress.co.uk

First published 2016
© Copyright: Richard Kell

The moral right of the author has been asserted.

© Cover photo, Statue of Shiva (Elephanta Island), by narrator

ISBN 978-1-910323-67-0

For Carolyn, Tim, and Shelagh
with grateful love

CONTENTS

I	FOREGROUND	1
	A Love Poem	3
	Making Word Gifts	4
	That Word	5
	Rhythm and Metre	6
	Home Sweet Home	7
	Morning	8
	Wet Day	9
	Resolution	10
	Tasks	11
	At My Desk	12
	Debussy	13
	Senile Song	14
	Second Childhood	15
	Itchy	16
II	MIDDLE GROUND	17
	The Dew Ponds	19
	A Dung Beetle in the Sahara	20
	Creatures Great and Small	21
	Practical Piety	22
	An Emblem	23
	Ball Lightning	24
	Bon Voyage	25
	By the Way	26
	Mythopoeia	28
	Etymology	29
	Performers	30
	High Places	31
	Gold	32
	Jade	33
	When?	34
	Two Heartless Men	35
	Shot at Dawn	36
	Frederick the Great	37

III	BACKGROUND	39
	Rhyme and Reason	41
	The Divided Will	42
	Do as You Would Be Done by	43
	An Elderly Reader	44
	For Any Young Enquirer	45
	The Progress of Wisdom	47
	To Giordano Bruno	48
	A Brief History of Religion	49
	Meteorological Theology	51
	Ancestral Spirits	52
	Know Thyself	53
	The Voice of Reason	55
	The Silence of Mystics	56
	God and the Scientists	58
	Red Fire Ants	60
	'Glory Be to God'	61
	Signals	63
	A Rueful Postscript	64
	Imagine	65
	A Modern Lesson	66
	Memento Mori	68
	For Realists	69
	The Dance of Shiva	70
	Good News	75

I

FOREGROUND

A LOVE POEM

(for Carolyn, Tim, Shelagh)

My daughters, my surviving son, forgive
the silences in my verse. One problem is
that what we feel for those with whom we live,
or used to live, creates complexities
not even prose would welcome. I could write
a simple lyric of praise for each of you,
heartfelt indeed, but at the risk of trite
conventional rhetoric. That wouldn't do!

Though you have much in common, you have each
your temperament, your talents. Poems try
quite often for big ideas but can't reach
(at least mine can't) the truth of 'you' and 'I'
and the full meaning of 'We love each other'.
You think of me and I of you; all four
remember a lost sibling, a lost mother.
No words can help us to accomplish more.

MAKING WORD GIFTS

I'll offer plain-speaking verse,
though my take on life may have a touch
of ironic humour, a smile melting a curse.
I'll frequently go for rhyme. That it's a crutch
(who coined that metaphor?) is bizarrely wrong.
Rhyming's not for the lame, it's like the task
of leaping hurdles, harder than running along
clear track though that's a skilled achievement too.
Sometimes I'll wear a mask,
an apt persona. More often I'll be me.
In either case I'll feel I'm addressing you
in a conversational way, although
it's impossible to see
more than a hint of what's going on below
pronominal surfaces. That prompts a turn
from poetry to ceramics. Though what I give
may lack the beauty of a Grecian urn,
it could be just as true. At least you'll have
a friendly pot – shape, colour, glaze
to cheer your heart a little on gloomy days.

THAT WORD

I've searched all morning, first my brain,
then the thesaurus, but in vain.
Lacking an adverb that combines
three nuances, the batch of lines
I've laboured on, so true and neat,
is torturingly incomplete.

Oh language, language, maddening gift
whose possibilities can lift
a poet's soul or lay it low!
My own, it seems, will rise and glow
only if I cut loose and coin
a word that makes three meanings join.

RHYTHM AND METRE

In the smooth train flowing
faster now, now slower,
we may become aware
of a humble drum
whose beat reminds us
of what we're riding on.

HOME SWEET HOME

(for Enid)

I'm on my own again,
back in my humble house,
feeling less man than mouse
with my anxious page, my pen.

Of course there's always wine
to keep me from going mad.
Too much of it would be bad
but it helps me shape a line.

Don't bother with my complaints.
It's you who'll bear the stress
of a disruptive mess
while the decorator paints.

How can I brood and sip
while, added to living rough,
you must be brave enough
to endure frail lungs, frail hip?

Couldn't I help, each day,
moving beds, tables, chairs,
spare you the awesome stairs,
bring you a takeaway?

You like a challenge, yes,
but I'd rather you feel free
to share the work with me
than suffer loneliness.

I hope, when the job's complete,
you'll judge it worth the pain,
feel truly at home again
and agree that home is sweet.

MORNING

(for Enid again)

Often there's nothing more delightful than bed,
particularly when we have to climb out of it.
But this is a day whose small hours
were sleepless, filled with the grit
of late life's anxiety and regret.
Now I've caught the delicious smell of bread
being baked by you, who are always up and busy
while I'm still down, calmly or fretfully lazy.
I'll lie here breathing it, maybe begin to drowse.

WET DAY

A crumple and crumble of thunder, then
the heavy relentless rain.
In ailing light
roofs are glistening,
leaves dripping.

How quickly the heart responds,
plucks from its repertoire of moods
melancholy, inertia.
I stay in my chair, under the weight
of wanting to do nothing.

RESOLUTION

It's time to get up and go.
Putting my book aside,
I imagine a man who's me
rising abruptly from the chair,
bracing his shoulders, saying 'I'm off'
and striding toward the door –
after which, loaded with far more no than yes,
I try to get inside him.

TASKS

Not a breath of wind.
Leafless trees quite still.
Seams of smooth grey cloud
and low-sun silver.

Calm, so calm, at one
with my sweet inertia.
Like sleep, almost like death.

A loveliness hard to resist,
hard to hate as I must
if I'm not to love myself
awake and idle.

AT MY DESK

It's windy this afternoon.
Foliage-filtered sunshine
has made, with scribbles of light
and shade across the page,
a dance of love and hate
inside my nervy brain.

Oh how you irritate,
dear leaves, dear sun! Forgive
what I'm about to do –
draw curtains, shut you out.
How else can I complete
this poem thanking you?

DEBUSSY

I loved, and even learned to play
in a far from perfect way,
his *Jardins sous la pluie* –
such a thrill of pattering notes
along the staves,
delight for thirsty roots,
for flowers and leaves.

If he had followed that
with *Jardins après la pluie*,
I wonder what
it would have sounded like
in helping us to see
sunlit calms where, gently,
ripples of air shake
raingleam to silver sparks.

Given how strangely,
magically, nature works
with art, might we have listened
to a rapt metaphor
telling how, after a downpour,
gardens glistened?

SENILE SONG

Less vital beings than worn machines
with nerves, we nod and smile.
How can the young know what it means
to feel each inch a mile?

SECOND CHILDHOOD

Another trudge, stick in hand.
Weary beat of heart, feet.

Passing a huge parked truck
I suddenly feel it an elder brother
loving and protective.

Astonished, amused, I imagine it,
when I've almost reached the medical centre,
thundering towards me at 50 miles an hour.

ITCHY

Rubbing on stone or wood can help the cows.
We use our fingers, furry folk their paws –
or sticks might soothe our backs with gentle claws.
For humankind at least, few treats can match
the tiny sensual heaven of a scratch.

II

MIDDLE GROUND

THE DEW PONDS

Wisdom and skill
made them thousands of years ago,
lined each cup with clay
on a bed of reeds or straw.
When summer pools below dried up,
these, high on the hill,
were filled at night with dew and mist,
so you'd be sure each day
to find them darkly glistening,
your tongue taste them cold and pure.

A DUNG BEETLE IN THE SAHARA

(from a David Attenborough film)

Ah, what a wondrous gift
from camel heaven! Having sniffed
its fine aroma she moulds it into a ball
and, still obeying instinct's call,
starts pushing it over the sand.
I'm with her all the way. I understand
and silently cheer her on. After a while,
mistress of rolling style,
she turns about and, with a will
to match her motor skill,
uses her back legs to advance
the precious load. But Chance
gives no more thought to beetle-being
than human or any other. She toils on, seeing
only the wrong way round, and sure enough,
abruptly the going gets rough.
From the crest of a dune she tumbles into a trough
along with the lovely dung. Will she give in?
Of course not: we see brave uphill work begin.
Oh dear, we see it begin again – and again –
and again… I recall the hellish pain
of Sisyphus. But that was endless. Thank heaven
(remote from the camel kind), after eleven
or possibly more attempts in the sun's oven,
she wisely calls it a day,
spreads self-preserving wings and flits away.

CREATURES GREAT AND SMALL

(from two wildlife films)

In South America the remains were found
of a grand constrictor, forty-eight feet long
and proportionately round.
It could squeeze to death, we're told, and swallow whole
the largest crocodile,
whose rugged carcass it would then digest
in a tank of acid. Not for a long while,
a year in fact, would the beast
require a comparable feast
and find another victim to encoil.

And here's a starfish creeping up
on limpets. If the prey is small
it will do its best to crawl
from danger's reach. A big one may escape
by slightly raising its inverted cup,
whose rim can then be used to scrape
a predatory arm.
With luck the echinoderm
will think it prudent to retreat
and poke around for less resistant meat.

PRACTICAL PIETY

The ample grace cup, passed from guest to guest,
was introduced, we're told,
by Margaret Atheling to enfold
the Scots, who liked to hit the trail
before each finished banquet had been blessed.

Benediction, they found, was bearable
with wine to follow. All parties now content,
it hardly mattered what the Lord might think
of diners who assent
to holiness when offered extra drink.

AN EMBLEM

I found, consulting a reference book to check
the meaning of *The anchor is apeak*,
'The cable of the anchor is so tight
that the vessel is drawn completely over it.'

Grip of iron and the urging of the ocean:
an image here for freedom and tradition?
I thought of all the souls who've felt the pain
of pulling hopelessly against a chain.

BALL LIGHTNING

Sometimes, when thunder's around,
a luminous sphere,
white or red, will move
spectral across the ground,
then suddenly disappear
without exploding. This
transient reminds me of
a fit of anger
that glows but brings no danger,
dying in renewed love,
a hug, a kiss.

BON VOYAGE

Believe it or not,
an expedition was fitted out
to find the Fountain of Youth
on one of the Bahama Islands.
Another of the demands
of romantic truth
was bleakly unfulfilled
time and again
for souls that primed themselves
to greet the end of the world
and waft to heaven.
How hope, springing eternal,
solves and dissolves,
as sound as the sound of a bell.

BY THE WAY

(1) Siege Towers

That belfries are so called
has nothing to do with chimes.
They resembled the *berfreis* hauled
to cities strongly walled
before stealth-bombing times.

(2) Faith

Daniel convinced the king
that Babylonian Bel
was an image, no true divinity.
Now believers cling
to the truth of the Holy Trinity,
virgin birth, heaven and hell.

(3) The Down of Up

It warms my heart
that these no longer endure
the wretchedness of a slum.
But Better can be a bitch.
When the poor stop being poor,
many, we notice, start
behaving like the rich.
Thrilled by their 'new lease',
forgivably they succumb
to the power of Mammon, become
consumerish, slack, obese.

(4) Beggars' Barm

Where the stream is partly blocked
foam gathers. It looks like yeast
but is 'beggarly': hunger's mocked
by the semblance of a feast.

MYTHOPOEIA

If we think of Gehenna, a gorge
outside Jerusalem,
perpetually in flame
as the place they tipped their trash
for incineration, then of the urge
humans have always had to blame
and punish, it's easy to see
how that dismal dump became
Hell, where sinners would gnash
their teeth eternally.

ETYMOLOGY

The vagaries of language show
how wildly thought and feeling flow.
Look up 'bully' and you'll discover
that once it meant a friend or lover.

PERFORMERS

Desultory: a nice
example of shifting sense.
The etymology gives
'leaping', from *desilire*,
and a desultor in Rome
was more than a fitful hopper.
Guiding a group of horses,
he'd spring from one to another
with hard-earned expertise.
In the big top's glowing cavern
rigour like that persists.
I'll botch a rhyme to code
how a slipshod word has mocked
the pride of circus artists.

HIGH PLACES

Hosea, Hezekiah and some others
vilified public worship in high places.
Pagans would caper there, around a pole
that pointed to or represented Baal.
Therefore those zealous leaders ruled out hills
as proper ground for holy rituals.
Sinai? One man alone had climbed to where
the true god thundered, frighteningly obscure.

All that aside, summits enchant us still.
Alone or not, we labour up the fell
till we have reached the top, and at the cairn
feel big and very small as we discern
bleak grandeur and a miniworld below.
They fill our hearts. We're human, we're in awe.

GOLD

Apart from its loveliness, I'm drawn by what
it meant throughout the ages. For example
El Dorado wasn't at first a place
the greedy conquistadores sought in vain,
but a supremo honoured by the Muiscas.
Every morning he had his body adorned
with powdered gold, and in a sacred lake
washed it off every evening. For his kind
the value of stuff that shared the sungod's colour
was spiritual, not commercial. Add to that
moral, aesthetic, political, romantic:
then you have age of gold, the golden calf,
the golden section and the golden mean,
the golden rule, the golden dome, 'silence
is golden', hearts of gold, gold torcs and bracelets,
gold jugs and plates, crowns, rods, chalices,
haloes…. But idealizing and craving
merged: the sacred and beautiful were worth
a fortune, gold was treasure. The grandest coins
were made of it, the gold standard governed
currencies, and Fort Knox, great box of bullion,
was guarded as grimly as the Pentagon.

JADE

Here I ignore the meanings 'worn out horse'
and 'objectionable woman', turn instead
to *piedra de ijada*, 'stone of the side'.
Spaniards believed that jade
possessed a magic force
to cure or prevent colic and even worse
complaints in the left or right
of the tender body. Amerindians wore
jade amulets against the bite
of snakes and against the curse
of gravel and epilepsy. Health apart,
the rich would purchase and adore
exquisite works of art
made of the gleaming mineral. So it goes:
earthy stuff cherished as something more,
to outwit the imps or charm the connoisseurs.

WHEN?

The Cape of Storms was the name
Bartholomew Dias gave it, but under
John of Portugal it became
Good Hope. Twins – for thunder
of sea and sky, though it dismays,
turns the mind at the same time
to help from heaven. I think of the days
of Nelson, days of the storming gun,
of his distant namesake, unarmed man
who indeed brought hope, and then
of what's happening now at the Cape,
corruption and violent power again,
massacre even. Is this the shape
of things to come, the same
(*Plus ça change...*) as it's always been –
Storm and Hope, each name
bound to the other, the age-old scene
of rock, wave, lightning and prayer for grace
from above, from the heart of the sky's menace?

TWO HEARTLESS MEN

'Well done! It's beautiful!'
cried Phalaris, chief bully,
when Perillos supplied
a fearsome brazen bull.
Offenders would be shoved inside
and under the beast's belly
a fire be lit.
'An oven fit for sin'
crowed Perillos. 'My best.'
'But can we be sure of it?'
the tyrant said. 'Fetch tinder.
We'll put it to the test.'
He made the artful smith get in
then cooked him to a cinder.

SHOT AT DAWN

(a reminiscence after 1918)

Deterrent? That's the judicial line.
Some officers, including me,
found it hard to agree or disagree,
but the act itself moved hearts like mine
to rebellious anger. – Paul
was in my platoon, a cheerful efficient man
well spoken of by all.
Serious too, and keen
to help a troubled mate.
We were astonished when he ran.
But who can judge the state
of another's nerves? Our ritual scene
at dawn was hard to bear,
but what about the storm from hell
two weeks before? – enough to scare
the toughest hero – shell on shell
scattering destruction with a burst
of thunder and scorching air.
Many, I know for sure, felt cursed
and close to running. You might say
Paul's terror was the same
or worse, but then what? 'Coward', to my way
of thinking, is a name
that's hollow. Seeing the firing squad take aim
I was sick at heart, and wishing it were true
that there's a Christ who knows us through and through.

FREDERICK THE GREAT

Monarchy, no. But here, against the odds,
was a gifted sovereign putting most of God's
appointees in the shade. On his accession
he promptly made his mark with the abolition
of torture, and a memorandum would plead
tolerance for all religions. How succeed,
being aesthete and philosopher, when you lead
an army? But he accomplished that as well,
having learned his regal duty, learned to quell
desires called self-indulgent. Rode at the head
of troops, won dazzling victories that would add
vast regions to his kingdom. Was that bad?
We think so now, but then you could be great
only by serving fearlessly a state
with a huge appetite for native soils
and an exchequer slavering for spoils.
Though autocrat, he gave the Enlightenment
as much alert devotion as he spent
on governing. His friend Voltaire would say,
speaking of how he portioned out his day,
'Sparta in the morning, Athens in the afternoon'.
Flautist, composer, he would make a tune
that Bach adorned in the 'Musical Offering'.
At Sans Souci he'd shed the role of king,
companion intellectuals. But they died
before him, left him lonely with his pride
in illustrious achievement. He had penned
a book against Machiavelli, and in the end
might claim he'd done his best to be humane,
fatherly, just. A creditable reign
as reigning goes, though he would favour lords,
invaluable on horseback with their swords,
while peasants were mostly slaves. – Monarchy, no.
But let's be fair, measure his kingly show

with dramas of 'Leader', 'Secretary', 'Chairman'.
There's no avoiding, it seems, a number one,
and if even the Boss of bosses made a mess
can't we call Frederick's try a near-success?

III

BACKGROUND

RHYME AND REASON

(for an imaginary correspondent)

You ask me what I'm trying to do –
poetry or verse? I'll leave to you
the separation of those two
and offer only this: I've spent
long hours defiantly intent
on making music from argument.

THE DIVIDED WILL

We say 'I did it against my will',
and that seems undeniable when,
for instance, there were bullying men
who threatened to punish or even kill
if we resisted. Force aside,
the effort of action when it's plain
that refusal – avoiding immediate pain –
might be more damaging to our pride
(which is sometimes altruistic), or
to our hope of smooth survival, than
engaging when we believe we can,
is different. But it's the clash before
we've chosen that bewilders me.
The inner fight between *will* and *won't*,
between *I want to* and *I don't*,
is like Tweedledum and Tweedledee
in absurd contention. Doing 'it'
can hardly have been against my will
if nobody threatened to hurt or kill,
so I have to assume a will was split
and twins did battle. How? Why?
Enlighten me! I've searched for ages,
without success, in thoughtful pages.
Many address the pronoun 'I',
the mysteries of the self, the will
to power, the death wish and so on,
but none the divided will. I've gone
through piles of print but am baffled still.

DO AS YOU WOULD BE DONE BY

To be nice to me she deprives herself.
Being nice to her I say
I'd rather she didn't deprive herself
but she says she's perfectly happy.
Then it occurs to me that if
she's perfectly happy depriving herself
the nicest thing I can do
is to let her do it.

Now she's perfectly happy
but after a while I'm not
because, being nice to her
so she can be nice to me,
I'm letting her deny herself
while she lets me indulge myself,
and that's a thought which thins
my pleasure and makes me feel not nice.

I turn this way and that,
amazed, hopelessly trapped
in the winsome logic of the Golden Rule.

AN ELDERLY READER

Revisiting a book
I read long years ago,
I see what care I took
in studying: going slow,
scribbling on every page
headings, marginal notes,
as if I had to assuage
a deep desire to *know*.
Now my memory yields
not even crude misquotes.
Did I walk too many fields,
explore too widely? No,
the trudge was good because
I learned some vital things
en route, e.g. that laws
of gods and priests and kings
were often quite absurd.
Their history's entertaining,
but in their time they stirred
horrific trouble, straining
obedience to despair.
So I'm glad I read this tome
and others with loving care.
Though details now look strange
I feel that I'm at home –
home on the cloudless range
where once I used to roam
and breathe the bracing air,
my mind going free and slow
as deer or buffalo
before the shooting there.

FOR ANY YOUNG ENQUIRER

What's real religion about? I know you know
it's not about saying your prayers or going to church,
confessing your sins, exchanging blow for blow
in sectarian violence. It's about the search
for truth – a troublesome concept (I know you know),
but vital to all from the scientist to the priest.
The wholly committed put aside weal and woe
except in their deep compassion for the least
of the creatures they share the planet with. Their God
isn't the one of popular art, a being
enthroned in heaven, with crown and robe and rod,
ruler of rulers. Truly religious seeing
begins with blindness, wonder, a humble sense
of mystery, deprecating the sacred verse
(God's message!), righteous outrage at the 'offence'
of a woman overcome by desire, the curse
and unmerciful punishment – even stoning to death.
'Truly religious'? Well, you can start with that,
but after you've rejected the shibboleth
and the concept of a heavenly autocrat
and all the other nonsense, it might be wise
to avoid confusion by saying, not 'religious',
but 'spiritual' or 'mystical'. – Many prize
the orthodox, conventional, prestigious
above the strange and loving. Jesus was
'despised and rejected of men' until a few
invented Christianity, noble cause
slowly corrupted as subtle doctrine grew
and his teaching was distorted. Through the ages
great cruelties were authorized in his name
by judges more like maniacs than sages.
'Spiritual' they said, but their real aim
(by most of them, let's allow, unrecognized)
was mainly political: to appease the 'King'

their king or pope relied on. Power disguised
as spirit, an old story! So let's not cling
even to 'spiritual', though it's an adjective
some contexts purify. No words will do
for how we approach the Void, the word we give
to God beyond comprehension – though this too,
like 'God' itself, is deeply tantalizing,
Plenum Void even worse! If language fails
in the heights of mysticism, that's not surprising,
since even within the day-to-day it veils
as much as it reveals. Scientists too
must be content with verbal approximation,
trying to express ideas that may be true
or mere imagining. Experimentation
and maths will tip the balance. It's the same –
'empirical' granted instead of 'experimental' –
with mystics. Trying to communicate, they name
something essential in terms of the accidental,
plunging into paradox. 'Plenum Void'
is a bit like 'quantum vacuum', name for a 'field'
that's far from empty. Should we be more annoyed
by the first than the second? What 'being' is revealed
in mystical 'vision', empirically outreaching
language? Quotation marks proliferate
(not *scare quotes* please!) because this isn't preaching.
Scientists beaver away; the mystics wait
(apart from scribbling) – hoping the 'dark night'
won't last too long – for the next affirmation,
'unknowing' certitude, 'self' lost in the 'light'
of the 'overself' beyond all definition.

THE PROGRESS OF WISDOM

Earthquakes were ascribed
by Eastern mythologies
to the stirring of outsize beasts –
tortoise, elephant, frog –
on whom the world rested.

For Romans they were caused
by the writhing limbs of giants
Jupiter buried beneath
high mountains: *cf* Vergil
on Enceladus under Etna.

Thunderbolts too… But the wrath
of Jehovah, once a weather god,
was tempest enough – and for him
came versions of hell more lurid
than presses composed of rock.

I think of poisonous minds
whose teaching poisons others,
then of mad moral myths
being gradually undone
by experiments and maths.

TO GIORDANO BRUNO

Forgive me that I've only read
about you. Since your day,
as long before, the human mind has bred
such swarms of speculation there's no way
the keenest polymath could study all.
I hope that it's enough for me to say
the Inquisition's cruelties appal
our modern hearts. But let me add,
if I'd been you, invited to retract
'unsound' beliefs, I doubt that I'd have had
courage like yours, to face the final act
('of faith') that put you to the stake,
the terrifying flames.
I love the deep conjectures that would shake
old certainties – anticipate the claims
of science and endorse the kind of thing
mystics had long been saying, though for most
these couldn't both be right: so many cling
firmly to either-or. No heavenly host
acclaimed you, earthlings do! The way you went
brought followers closer to enlightenment –
and what more could they ask,
facing, it seems, a never-ending task.

A BRIEF HISTORY OF RELIGION

(one version)

In primal pantheons the deities
belonged to earth and sky, were sensed in trees,
rivers, mountains, lightning, intoxicants.
Their moods were what the gifted hierophants
tried hard to manage. They had nothing to do
with morality. Though this was sacred too,
its root was social custom, which the ancestral
spirits were guardians of – until a trivial
god emerged with a list of rights and wrongs.
He wasn't mentioned in the rapturous songs
about fire, thunder, warfare, wine. But then
somehow the social earnestness of men,
kept firm by praise and condemnation, started
mixing with thoughts not only of the departed
but also of divinities, who became –
though their behaviour was pretty much the same
as that of humans, from sordid to sublime –
enraged by immoral conduct. For example
Zeus, though a dodgy despot, had a temple
where Hellenes, neither lunatics nor dolts,
grovelled before him, fearing thunderbolts
if he should find them wanting. Yahweh then,
also a weather god, delivered ten
commandments and became the Only One,
father and wrathful king but, even so,
a hazy Being we mortals couldn't know,
a mystery so far beyond our reach
that only the letters YHWH,
bare script, could represent him. His devotees
attacked the unrighteous mythifiers of trees
and bulls and genitalia. In our age
mythologies – each the true one – still engage
in holy strife, their rituals tied in

with politics et cetera. Cash and spin
play worthy roles, and after the crusades
we've rockets, bombs and mines instead of blades
to honour gods whose bolts once terrified
the clans, foreshadowing faithful genocide.

METEOROLOGICAL THEOLOGY

What made the people cower,
though rarer violence could be worse,
was the thunderstorm. Each fierce
quick bolt was like an angry curse,
a warning token of the power
of sky gods: Baal, Zeus-Jupiter, Thor,
even Yahweh before his great
promotion. – Understandable,
but infinitely sad as well
when priests conceived the cruellest fate:
eternal punishment for sin
by heaven's fire, sublimely thin
up there, enriched when piped to hell.

ANCESTRAL SPIRITS

Believe, like dear old Aunt?
No, I simply can't.
How could I even start
when science has dumped Descartes?

But what if they do exist,
floating around our heads
like fine invisible mist
while we're in or out of our beds?

Watching our lives, aware
of all the good and bad
impulsions *they* once had,
how deeply do they care?

Do they sigh? laugh? sneer?
If they could, would they shed a tear?
Can they help us to be nice,
prepare us for Paradise?

Questions, questions. Best
not ponder them at all,
lest we become obsessed
with mysteries that appal.

KNOW THYSELF

I wasn't meant to hear when someone hissed
'escapist'. I was barely twenty then.
A word can be more powerful than a fist,
and that one, saying 'feeble specimen',
seemed full of insight. Though I've worked quite hard
at all my duties, something has been wrong.
It might be put like this: two wills have jarred,
a weak contending always with a strong,
escapist versus realist. Does that
make sense? No matter. Something undermined
parts of the earnest life I laboured at.
I wasn't what I seemed to be: my kind
were slack romantic dreamers. I had loved
Davies ('What is this life…') and Stevenson
('Give to me the life…'), dropouts who roved
the countryside. The trouble was, they'd done
what I could never do, both living rough,
both tramps, one with a donkey. Who was I
to link myself with wanderers so tough?
Did heartache give me any right to sigh
for simple ways? But all of us – it's true
though tediously trite – are what we are.
I loved to walk where gorse and heather grew,
loved rivers, woodland, seawaves, and the far
horizons, real or metaphysical,
that wistful verse and music let me see.
Then back to work, the restless double will,
the blessing and the curse of being 'me'.
Quotation marks because I read that Hume
and Gautama and neuroscientists
have doubted something most of us assume.
The sense of self, the wilful 'I', persists
but may be mental trickery. Who knows?
Anyway here we are, I, you, her, him –

or so we unavoidably suppose –
living no more by reason than by whim,
our differences the fancywork of fate
or chance or (is it credible?) of God.
At least we're all alike in love and hate.
The saint, the rogue, the genius and the clod
are thrown together in an epic filled
with tragedy and farce, each playing a role
some crazy cosmic pseudo-bard has willed,
each burdened with what seems a self or soul.
Though all agree that 'Know thyself' is wise,
I'm wondering if, besides the obvious –
that lives are shaky when they're built on lies –
it's hinting there's no referent for 'us'
unless (add 'Thou art That') a strange disguise.

THE VOICE OF REASON

Let's favour reason in daily affairs,
in psychology, politics, morals…
That's best for being humane,
getting along, reducing quarrels.
But reason itself declares
it can only go so far,
there's something it can't explain.
"I can tell you about a star"
it says, "an atom, a cell, a brain;
but we've heard of a strange experience
beyond the range of sense
(both meanings), therefore beyond
my clear-headed competence.
Mystical: that's a term, I know,
educated people are fond
of deriding, but I think they're wrong.
Into the Void, a few have long
asserted, my words can't hope to go.
Fine! As well as the rational there's
the suprarational. Human affairs,
improved by me, would be better still
if people could learn to meditate
without the grip of self-centred will
and its common language – could reach a state
where the world we call the everyday,
of sights and sounds and all the rest,
being Maya though 'real', falls away.
Most scientists have no truck with this,
a claim their expertise can't test.
Einstein was different I'm glad to say:
he believed in reason but also bliss."

THE SILENCE OF MYSTICS

Mystical knowledge? Impossible, you say.
I think you're right, but perhaps you don't know why.
Knowledge depends on subject and object, *I*
perceiving *it*, whatever it happens to be
in the world where language points
to things and persons real for you and me.
It's here that speaking counts.
Mystics tell us again and again
that the words for our reality can't begin
to describe the one it veils. There
(what does *that* mean?) they've no desire
for meanings. But the rest of us,
excluded, bewildered, curious,
plead for description, so they use
words that are useless, including those
the religious use. We 'know', they say,
God or Spirit or Void – yet knower and known
vanish, they tell us, when they're shown
whatever they're shown, so it makes more sense
to honour their strange experience
by choosing a metaphor:
'enlightenment' or 'illumination' or
'awakening'. And who's to say,
given the mystical way
and the scientific – each
believing it can reach
a reality of its own, and both
experiential, empirical – that truth
is reserved for only one? Einstein could call
mystic illumination 'most beautiful'
and even 'the dower of all
true science'. – Vaughan could write
'There is in God (some say)
a deep but dazzling darkness'. No wonder light

is a metaphor we've chosen to convey
what seekers hope for. God's another word –
so vague and, offering lucent black, absurd –
that's faithful to unknowing when it's used
by mystics, not the chaptered but confused
'faithful', with their schools
all bickering while convinced that moral rules
came to mankind from Him.
Dear *sapiens,* how clever and how dim!
Science and mysticism are the best
we've yet achieved, I think. How else arrest
our glorious career,
helped on by atavistic pride and fear
and greed and all the rest,
towards chaos and extinction? But scientists
don't claim to *know:* each theory persists
until another proves more fertile. Nor
do mystics, though their use of metaphor –
'spirit' instead of 'energy' for instance,
or 'light' and then 'illumination' –
serves a purpose different from that of science,
one that has nothing to do with cerebration.
For them unknowing and knowing are the same,
each a concept useless for what they claim.

GOD AND THE SCIENTISTS

Dawkins' *The God Delusion*
or Davies' *The Mind of God?*
Though some may think it odd,
I came to the conclusion
that both of them were right.
The Gods on which they shone
their powerful streams of light
are very different: one
a superhuman father
whose methods can appal
his children, and the other
impersonal, mystical,
ineffable. The first
has lots of priestly schools
whose brethren are immersed
in dispute: moral rules
and problematic dogma
simmer their brains. The second,
for church folk an enigma,
a kind of fog that's thickened
by vapours from the East,
appealed to Albert Einstein,
who wasn't in the least
an otherworldly man.
'The mystical,' he wrote,
'is the dower of all true science' –
an aphorism remote
from the sayings of commonsense
and of erudition too
when they're firmly orthodox.
For Dawkins it's untrue,
unfit for his tidy box.
But Davies, I'm glad to say,
considers that, although

a perfect theorem shows
as much as reason can
uncover and define,
there's more the mind of Man
can never hope to know
unless by going the way
deep mysticism goes,
where termless meanings shine.

RED FIRE ANTS

Voracious and innocently lethal
as fire itself, they cluster,
after their bites have scared
a cayman mother away,
to gorge on her hatching babies,
who strive in baffled terror to shake them off.

All is well says Mother Nature,
superlative calculator.
Enough young caymans escape
to become, like humans, high-powered predators,
and enough ants are cancelled
by decapitating flies.

Sometimes, looking down at the great lady,
God says things like this:
'My dear, you're doing a marvellous job keeping
our crowded globe tidy.'

'GLORY BE TO GOD'

How I loved Hopkins then! – revelled with him
in dappled things, the lovely behaviour
of silk-sack clouds, dragonflies drawing flame,
the falcon's hurl and gliding...
With him I worshipped God in Nature,
but only romantically, not
bothering with the dogma-laden, priestly
grounding of his vision.

One day a clever undergraduate friend
who was studying law shattered with one blow
the trust I shared with the poet.
Nature? All right, a harmless
personification. But godly revelation?
Clouds, sunlit or not, were simply clouds,
dapple was dapple... I turned away sad and silent.

On a later day I went to the flicks instead of
attending a freshman lecture.
Nature's Half Acre, before the feature film,
did even more than my friend's sharp intellect
to disenchant me when the camera peered
enquiringly among grassblades, flowers, leaves.
After our nursery rhymes we'd had
    'You are nearer God's heart in a garden
    Than anywhere else on earth',
'The Lord is my shepherd', 'All things bright and beautiful'.
I'd walked with ignorant joy in meadow and woodland,
lingered by river or pond, delighting
in bird, fish, insect, and their snug retreats.

Nature's Half Acre smashed
all that, replaced the rapturous lie with fact.

In childhood the little we'd known about predation
had been well wrapped and stowed away.
As for the expedients of the ichneumon wasp,
of the cuckoo loved for her mellow fluting,
these, along with the disagreeable thought
of Man as top predator,
were extras to be inflicted years after
I suffered – escapist in a smoky womb –
close-ups of creeping killers, of jaws
and sting-ducts engaged, with innocent expertise,
in the callous competition that Mother Nature
so ably managed on behalf of
the Lord God who made them all –
ants and hornets, beetles and spiders, birds
(whose song, that rhyme had carolled, was 'for mirth'),
and us, who kill each other as well as them.

I still love earth, sky, ocean – more wisely now.
I still love Hopkins' poems including
the vision aglow in the language, but
that vision is only his, no longer mine.
His lines had never hung on our walls
beside the pokerwork jingles, but they too
left out the unholy details
that pierced my heart one truant afternoon.

SIGNALS

Physicists can trace,
in cloud or bubble chamber,
particles they've no hope
of seeing even through
a powerful microscope.

Scanning neuronal lace
when subjects get a cue
to anticipate or remember
anxiety, grief, joy,
neuroscientists find
which parts are flitted through
by waves involving 'mind'.

And what do *we* employ?
The look on someone's face,
a word, a grunt, a gesture,
so easy to misread.
When all the text allows
are these, is it any wonder
companionship can lead
to silences and rows?

A RUEFUL POSTSCRIPT

(to my poem 'Signals')

Advances in the lab become a curse
as soon as they start messing with my verse.
What scans were widely thought to demonstrate –
that a thrill and a piece of brainstuff correlate –
has now been judged fallacious, like the claim
that for some inclination we can blame
or praise a single gene. Since keeping up
is also being a bit behind, we sup
with the devil when we favour an alliance
between the powers of poetry and of science.

IMAGINE

I like *New Scientist*,
but sometimes it makes me feel as though
I'm falling into a pit
or adrift in the twilight zone.
A title promises wonders not to be missed,
and here's what you get below:
'Imagine printing out a paper computer
and tearing off a corner
so someone else can use a part of it...
In twenty years you will really be able to hit
Print and make yourself a mobile phone.'

That's the beginning and ending
of a recent report. Plainly
our species is ascending,
but in ways that make me feel I'm still mainly
an ape. Observers enjoy the show
as I happily tear a sheet
of paper to pieces, which I eat
like forest leaves. But alas, no:
I'm a literate human with a text
providing a more elusive treat.
My mind is weirdly hazed, you might say hexed.

A MODERN LESSON

Life versus death. Life good,
death bad. Life often bad,
but good compared with death.
Decay, of course, death's mate,
and both of them destroyers,
agents of half our woes.
So runs the enduring myth,
along with God and Fate
and for some, still, the Devil.
All understandable,
so I'm not going to cavil.
But beings endowed with life
are the top destroyers – from
the tiniest of bugs
to men with gun or knife.
Dying is then life's dregs
draining away, breath
failing when lungs become
helpless. In short, death
does nothing. It's the state
of a creature fatally hurt
by the micro- or macroscopic
behaviour of some other,
or by molecules that poison –
unless a life that shone
with steady flame has burned
right down: a candle wick,
its long work done.
I see no hooded scyther!
And our companion topic,
decay – what can we find
in that? Rocks weather:
their substance is eroded
by force of water and wind.
A piece of iron's corroded

by contact with oxygen.
When autumn leaves wither
we're witnessing an end
that's part of a vital process.
And life persists again
throughout the rotting mess
of a dead body. Within
the putrid flesh there are lots
of lively things going on –
or there's one thing, you might say:
voracious feeding on guts
that used to process food.
Predators – protozoon
to larva – gorge on prey
progressively less tiny,
and isn't eating 'good'?
A long story... What's left
is clean, soft, grainy
and fertile, 'nature's gift'
to the gardener, who'll cultivate
plants for the human gut.
So shouldn't we all shut up
about life versus death and decay?
Let's think instead about change
endless and intricate: changing
formations of energy ranging
from (maybe) superstrings
to all the visible things
we call the world: stars,
planets, mountains, oceans,
animals, buildings, cars,
spacecraft and space stations,
all the stuff that flows
from the first explosion. Whatever
realities our equations
and probes can't hope to discover
'God' only knows.

MEMENTO MORI

Saying 'I'm off to bed',
worn out when day is done,
we give no thought at all
to dreams, happy or sad:
we only want to fall
into pure oblivion.
So why are we afraid
of dying? That's slightly mad.
Or is it rational?
No longer simian,
we're creatures who have had
to think, to brood upon
the living and the dead.
But then our gifts have made
fables and lodged them deep
in theologies. – Instead
of hollow skull I'll use
a disillusioned brain,
remember without dread
our common fate, the sleep
whose gift will be to lose
a self and all its pain.

FOR REALISTS

What could be more welcome than
the void of dreamless sleep,
nature's kindliest form
of brief oblivion.
In this we elude the swarm
of demons that haunts our days,
often our nights as well
if it flits among counted sheep
then hangs around to craze
dreaming with sparks from hell.
Some Hindu sages teach
that dreamless sleep is one of the ways
of approaching Brahman – a pleasing
idea beyond the reach
of my intellect. I'll settle for
a godless kind of easing
all understand: escape from war
within the self and among
so many selves. I'll even sing,
as very few have sung,
in praise of the final sleep.
'Death, where is thy sting?'
 – a modern version. Who can deny,
in a world where suffering
makes billions curse or weep,
it will be good to die
and enter the mindless deep.

THE DANCE OF SHIVA

(for John Lucas)

(1)

I'm a mild fellow really:
it's only when I'm writing
I get a little surly
and do some verbal smiting.

Because my heart is gentle,
the ills I see around me
are apt to turn me mental,
to frighten and confound me.

It gives me quite a pain
that millions glorify
as *lila* a domain
where so much goes awry.

'Divine play'? Any god
who finds disaster fun
is a sadistic sod
I feel we ought to shun.

'But it's all *maya*' says
the guru. 'When the spell
dissolves, a heaven appears
that seemed an earthly hell.'

How marvellous it will be,
if I achieve that state,
to discover I can see
with love what now I hate.

Behold, I will have altered
from a dim pathetic creature
who often sighed and faltered
to a potential preacher

strangely uplifted by
the way that thugs behave,
the fact that thousands die
in the earthquake or the wave,

poverty, war, disease,
an orphaned child's dismay,
the torturer's expertise,
the predator with its prey.

In bliss I'll contemplate
a world it's Shiva's joy
to playfully create
and playfully destroy.

Instead of cursing Chance
when I misunderstood,
I'll praise the eternal dance,
assured that evil's good.

Then, putting pen to paper,
I'll always be discreet:
that paradisal caper
will keep my verses sweet.

(2)

'Mild fellow', fellow-dunce,
have you misunderstood
the myth of Shiva's Dance?
Does it say evil's good?

For me it's still obscure
though pondered since my teens.
Are even gurus sure
of what the image means?

They might remind us how
the ancient Hindus guessed,
if that's the word, what now
equations have expressed:

destruction and re-creation,
new world replacing old,
in popular translation
the Big Bounce, not foretold

but 'allowed' by calculus.
(Did any dream the ascent
of maths from the abacus
to this great instrument?)

World after world, or one
dying to a final void,
everything nature's done
entropically destroyed?

But put aside coming, going.
What I now have in mind
is creating and destroying,
though opposites, intertwined.

Is ingrained conflict – not
an eternal enterprise,
a world's recycling – what
the godly dance implies?

Death is a lifeless state
caused most of all by life:
mosquito, microbe, hate
equipped with gun or knife.

Add innocent predation,
from colony to pack
ferocious adaptation,
survival by attack.

Shape things of iron or steel
and not crush rock? You can't!
Even to make a meal
violates beast or plant.

When wreck, plague, massacre come –
sure signs of godly wrath
or star-told fate for some –
no killing's done by death.

We see one world, no other,
and what it seems to show
is opposites together
in a troubled, troubling flow

we magnify as Good
with Evil. But when the spell
dissolves it's understood,
perhaps, that all is well:

that contraries are blended
for texture of the One,
like quantal strife transcended
as a gold-glowing sun.

Among the myths a few
are fine as any gem,
fantastically true.
Is Shiva one of them?

GOOD NEWS

One day, in twenty-four-sixty-five,
there was a strange event.
Everything stopped for a moment
though everyone stayed alive.
All humans had the supreme
experience called nirvana, and
a moment later, as though
awaking from a dream –
which it hadn't been, but a glow
of pure reality no one could understand –
they found themselves transformed,
serene and full of love.
                    They'd already warmed
a lot to one another, and been amazed
by what had occurred before.
People must have been crazed,
they said, to have hated so much, to have waged war
as tribes and nations, for territory
and then imperial glory –
not to mention (and so to mention!)
petty familial quarrels
and neighbourly dissension,
anger over religious beliefs, morals,
political preferences. They understood
that words like bad and good
have nothing at all to do with godly laws.
They knew about their descent
from apes; that ravenous jaws
had evolved by natural selection
for eating and hence survival;
also that, after millennia, 'good' had meant
a struggle against the 'evil'
of brute desire, towards the perfection
called holiness. But none of that had worked.

Within the ideals lurked
atavistic realities. Greed
and fear and the will to power
were wrapped in this or that shining creed
protected by church or battle tower
or, usually, both.
                    And so the strife went on,
with patches of peace. Though kindly things were done
in the name of charity, still the poor were poor,
wretched, resentful. Some thinkers, good and wise,
dreaming perfection, spoke or wrote
inspiringly, but resolutions
and deep reforms brought practices remote
from what was longed for. Lies
appeared as truth, solutions
produced new problems. Still the fruit
of human-ness was acid at its core,
though worshippers could adore
a loving Father-God, subjects extol
fatherly kings, cathedrals and castles soar –
voices too, their music lifting the soul
towards Heaven, where angels sang.
But also there was a domain
for impenitent sinners, where a gang
of devils inflicted eternal pain
by the wholly 'just' decree
of that 'merciful' Father-God,
whose rulings could not be changed
by any sorrowful plea
once he had raised his rod
against daughter or son estranged.
    It dawned on thoughtful minds that all this stuff
was delusion. Some said a calculated bluff
by governors and their priests
to keep the people obedient out of fear –
Heaven modelled on castle, orchard, feasts,

Hell on the dismal dungeon. Others agreed
to the model but not the intent: you couldn't be clear
about motives, even your own. But whatever the seed,
a fantastic tree had grown, imagination's
logic had made the branches and the leaves
of a myth from which theologies would weave
with rational logic subtle complications
provoking scholastic disagreement. Then
came dogma, then cries of 'Heresy!'. Cruel men
professing love used rack and red-hot iron
to urge repentance that would bring salvation.
Those who resisted to the end would burn
in the market place and by the Father's will
be damned for ever – or, in later years,
be loved as glorious martyrs. Blood would spill
for centuries, mothers' tears
be shed for sons who fought in the name of faith
for one or another version of a myth.
    In later times, great revolutions
altered millions of lives. Though driven at first
by doctrines that were pure,
humanitarian, full of hope,
they led to terror, to lethal persecutions
ordered by minds no longer immersed
in traditional make-believe but grimly sure
as those of God-bent king and pope.
    All this was a blend
of ancient history and legend
by twenty-four-sixty-five,
before that wonderful event,
global nirvana. A few
had found themselves alive
after the final war – well meant
as usual by allies and enemies
when fear and hatred grew
again, after a freeze,

to explosive heat, this time richly expressed
by nuclear power. Some who survived felt blest
as people do when Fate
or God or God-knows-what
grants a reprieve although their lot
couldn't be worse. Many would still mate
and produce children, but Earth was ravaged,
the man-built mostly rubble, competition
for food and shelter savage.

    A few got round to thinking 'Why, why?
Isn't it better to die
than face, year after year, this slow attrition
of body and mind?' But a poet had once said
'Hope springs eternal in the human breast'.
True, if only because
we hate the thought of dying. Now a shred
of hope carried a seed that became a tree
spreading from East to West.
Its branches were kindly laws
put forth by general choice and free
from penalties. Everyone understood
they had no guidelines for being good
that weren't quite simple. There'd been a time,
scholars reported, when from East to West
wise men had offered the paradigm
'Do as you would be done by', the only test
for thoughts and deeds called moral. That,
in the twenty-fifth century, people knew,
meant *social* – nothing more
and nothing less. No autocrat
in heaven or earth could tell them what was true
or false, or could involve them in a war
to further his obsessions.

                      I have to cut
a long long story short. I won't pretend
there were no problems, but on the whole

they were solved without rancour, since the goal
was always to treat one's neighbour as one's friend.
People saw themselves now as members of
a species — not a tribe, a race, a nation.
They did their best to empathize and love.
Difficult, to the point of self-negation!
But that's what happened. By the year
twenty-four-sixty-five
everyone was ready. Most of the fear
and craving and anger that remained
after millennia — from self-centredness,
individual then collective — had drained
away. Then came nirvana: no more stress,
no more inner or outer conflict. Yes,
it's hard to credit. Even
a Buddhist wouldn't believe
that all the people across the world could achieve
in a moment, or be 'given',
such harmony.
                I too would be sceptical
if I hadn't heard these facts from a timeless Muse.
She said 'Don't worry: all is well
in a world you'll never see.
I want us to make a poem called Good News.
Write plainly. Be true to me.'